MARYLAND

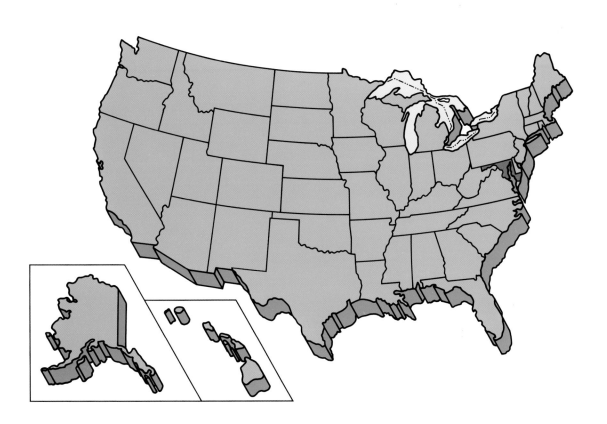

MARYLAND

Joyce Johnston

Lerner Publications Company

Cover photograph courtesy of U.S. Naval Academy.

The glossary that begins on page 68 gives definitions of words shown in **bold type** in the text.

LIBRARY OF CONGRESS
CATALOGING-IN-PUBLICATION DATA
Johnston, Joyce.
    Maryland / Joyce Johnston.
      p. cm. — (Hello USA)
    Includes index.
    Summary: Introduces the geography, history, people, industries, and other highlights of Maryland.
    ISBN 0-8225-2713-8 (lib. bdg.)
    1. Maryland—Juvenile literature.
[1. Maryland.] I. Title. II. Series.
F181.3.J64 1991
975.2—dc20   91-14456
                      CIP
                      AC

CONTENTS

The Wye Oak

Did You Know . . . ?

☐ Wye Mills, Maryland, boasts the largest white oak tree in the United States. More than 400 years old, the Wye Oak is taller than a 10-storied building.

☐ You can walk across Maryland in less than 30 minutes! The state is only 1.5 miles (2.4 kilometers) wide at its narrowest point.

The first successful hot-air balloon flight in the United States was launched in Maryland in 1784. The balloon's basket carried 13-year-old Edward Warren of Baltimore.

Jousting

The Baltimore and Ohio (B&O) Railroad, which was founded in Maryland, built the first passenger train in the United States. The train could travel as fast as 20 miles (32 km) per hour—about as fast as some bicyclists pedal.

Maryland's official state sport is jousting. In the joust, two people mounted on horses try to knock each other to the ground with long lances, or spears. Each year Maryland holds a state jousting tournament.

7

A Trip Around the State

Day after day, the waves of the Chesapeake Bay lap against Calvert Cliffs. The waves slowly grind down the walls of the cliffs, uncovering ancient teeth, bones, and shells buried in the rock. These fossils come from sharks and whales that swam the oceans millions of years ago.

Calvert Cliffs is in Maryland, the eighth smallest state in the United States. Maryland, a southern state, lies on the East Coast. The Mason-Dixon Line—the historical boundary between the North and the South—divides Maryland from its northern neighbor, Pennsylvania.

A crowd of ducks and swans *(below)* enjoys the Chesapeake Bay. Hundreds of fossils line Calvert Cliffs *(right).*

Tall grasslike plants thrive in Maryland's wetlands.

Maryland has a winding southern border, marked mostly by the Potomac River. Washington, D. C., the nation's capital, sits just north of the river. South of the Potomac lie Virginia and West Virginia. Delaware and the Atlantic Ocean are Maryland's neighbors to the east.

Maryland has three land regions—the Coastal Plain, the Piedmont, and the Appalachian Highlands. The Coastal Plain stretches across eastern Maryland and is nearly sliced in two by the Chesapeake Bay. The land east of the bay is called the Eastern Shore. The plain gradually rises from flatlands to low hills. **Marshes,** or wetlands, line the bay. Pine forests are found throughout the plain.

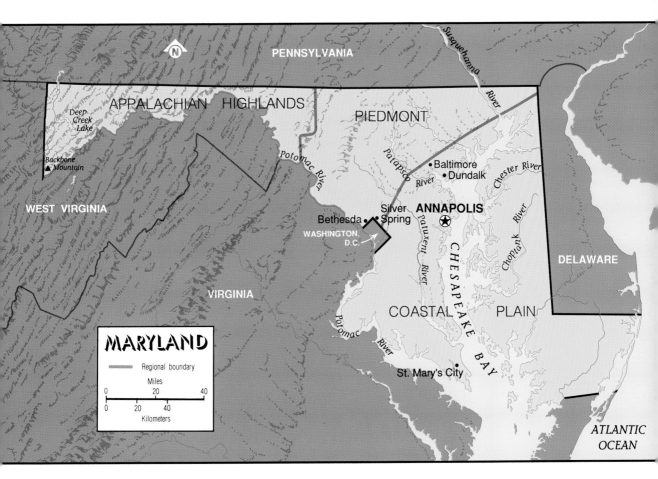

MARYLAND

Regional boundary

Miles
0   20   40

0   20   40
Kilometers

Cows graze in the Piedmont region.

The Piedmont region stretches across the middle of Maryland from north to south. Low, wooded hills rise gently from the region's wide valleys. Dairy farms, as well as fields of wheat and corn, are common sights in the Piedmont.

The Appalachian Highlands rise beyond the Piedmont in the westernmost part of the state. Two mountain ranges, the Alleghenies and the Blue Ridge, cross the highlands. Their steep ridges and peaks are part of the Appalachian Mountains, an ancient mountain chain that stretches all the way from Canada to Alabama.

The Blue Ridge Mountains are named for the blue haze that hangs over the mountain forests. Backbone Mountain, a ridge of the Alleghenies, rises to 3,360 feet (1,024 meters) and is the tallest point in Maryland.

Not far from Backbone Mountain lie the quiet waters of Deep Creek Lake, the largest lake in Maryland. Deep Creek, like all lakes in Maryland, is artificial. It was created when a small dam was built to block the passage of a waterway.

Deep Creek Lake, in western Maryland, spans 4,000 acres (1,620 hectares).

More than 50 rivers flow through Maryland to the Chesapeake Bay. The Potomac, Patuxent, and Patapsco rivers drain much of the state. The Susquehanna, which runs through northeastern Maryland, brings water into the Chesapeake from as far away as New York. The Chester and Choptank rivers wind their way through the forests, farmlands, and marshes of the Eastern Shore.

Rivers flowing into the Chesapeake Bay cut up Maryland's shoreline.

14

The black-eyed Susan is Maryland's state flower.

The streams and rivers that flow across western Maryland toward the Chesapeake Bay cross what is called the Fall Line. Streams and rivers form waterfalls and rapids as they tumble over the Fall Line—that is, from the rocky soils of the Piedmont down to the loose soils of the Coastal Plain.

The Chesapeake Bay and the Atlantic Ocean affect weather conditions in the coastal areas of the state. In the summer, the waters absorb heat, cooling the land around them. In the winter, they become huge radiators, giving back the heat collected in the summer and warming the land nearby. Away from the bay and the ocean, in the Piedmont and the Appalachians, winter temperatures are generally cooler than in the Coastal Plain.

In the fall, leaves turn from green to brilliant yellows, oranges, and reds.

Baby opossums stay very close to their mother.

The mild winters of the Eastern Shore attract many kinds of birds. Nearly one million ducks and geese from the northern United States and Canada spend winters in Maryland's marshy areas. During the winter and summer, oysters, crabs, and clams live in the bay. White-tailed deer, raccoons, red and gray foxes, and opossums roam the state's forests year-round.

Forests cover almost half of Maryland. Loblolly pine, sweet gum, Spanish oak, and bald cypress trees grow near the wetlands in southern Maryland. In the northwest, evergreen trees such as white pine and hemlock fill the cool mountain forests. Partly because of the variety of plants and animals in this tiny state, Maryland is sometimes called America in Miniature.

17

Maryland's Story

On almost any map of Maryland, you can find traces of the first peoples who lived there. Chesapeake, Wicomico, Catoctin, Allegheny, Assateague—all of these and many more of Maryland's place-names come from Native American, or Indian, words.

Indians probably came to North America from Asia about 10,000 years ago. Eventually, some Indians reached the forests of what we now call Maryland and hunted deer. These people didn't live in cities and towns. They moved around, always looking for sources of food.

Later Indians lived in small houses called lodges. Hunters caught their prey in traps. They fished the rivers and the Chesapeake Bay with nets, sinkers, and hooks. The Indians also traded food and blankets with neighboring groups to the north and south.

Native American lodges

18

By the early 1600s, several tribes were living near the Chesapeake Bay. The Piscataway made their homes in what would become southern Maryland. The Nanticoke, Choptank, Assateague, and Pocomoke had territories on the Eastern Shore. The Susquehanna settled at the head of the bay.

Around this time, explorers from the British Isles crossed the Atlantic Ocean and landed on the shores of North America. The seafarers claimed much of the coast—including the Chesapeake Bay area—for Great Britain.

In 1632 the king of Britain, Charles I, granted part of the bay area to a British nobleman, Lord Baltimore. The king named this land Mariland (later spelled Maryland), after his wife, Queen Henrietta Maria.

Queen Henrietta Maria

Maryland's first settlers arrived from Great Britain in two ships—the *Ark* and the *Dove*—after a long, rough journey.

Lord Baltimore was to start a **colony,** or settlement, of British people in Maryland. In the spring of 1634, two British ships sailed into the Chesapeake Bay and up the Potomac River. They carried about 150 people who planned to make Maryland their new home.

Maryland's colonists soon found a natural harbor—a place where ships could dock easily—along the Potomac River. The newcomers began building houses, a fort, and a church near the harbor. They called their new settlement St. Mary's City.

Leonard Calvert greets an Indian aboard the *Ark*.

Among the settlers was Leonard Calvert, a brother to Lord Baltimore. Calvert became the colony's first governor. He allowed people to choose their own religion—a freedom they did not have in Great Britain. Because Calvert permitted freedom of religion, people from other colonies and from Britain flocked to Maryland.

Many Indians were friendly to the British settlers, trading furs and food for tools and cloth. The Indians taught the newcomers how to plant corn, a skill that saved the settlers from starvation. To make sure they would have food during the upcoming winter, the settlers worked hard planting crops.

Looking for a way to make money, some settlers planted tobacco. Farmers could sell much of this crop to Britain, where the dried leaves were used as medicine. With the profits from tobacco sales, the colonists began to build **plantations,** or large farms, to grow even more tobacco.

The colonists sold their tobacco crops to Great Britain.

Plantations began to gobble up land, and Indian families were forced to leave their homes in Maryland. The Indians moved first to the colonies of Pennsylvania and New York and finally to Canada. Many Indians who stayed died from diseases brought by the colonists. By 1750 almost no Indians remained in Maryland.

23

Great Britain wasn't the only European nation to send settlers to North America. France had colonies too. In the mid-1700s, the two countries fought for control of the land around the **Great Lakes**. This conflict is known as the French and Indian War, so named because many Indians sided with the French.

To pay for the war, the British government taxed sugar, tea, newspapers, playing cards, and other goods the colonists imported from Britain. The settlers were angry and bought as little as they could from Britain. The British government dropped some taxes but continued to tax tea.

Settlers who were angry about the British tax on tea cheered as the *Peggy Stewart* was set on fire in the harbor at Annapolis. The ship carried 2,000 pounds (908 kilograms) of British tea.

The colonies wanted freedom from British rule, so they could make their own laws. Soldiers from each of the 13 colonies formed the Continental army. By the end of 1775, Britain and its 13 North American colonies were locked in a war—the American War of Independence, also called the Revolution.

Very little fighting took place in Maryland during the Revolution. However, the colony sent a group of soldiers, called the Maryland Line, to join the Continental army. In battles against the British, the Maryland Line was rarely beaten. One of Maryland's nicknames, the Old Line State, comes from the colony's dependable troops.

On July 3, 1776, the people of Maryland declared that their colony was independent of Great Britain. The next day, four Marylanders were among the colonists who signed the Declaration of Independence. This letter announced that the 13 colonies no longer belonged to Britain.

The Maryland Line wore bright clothing.

25

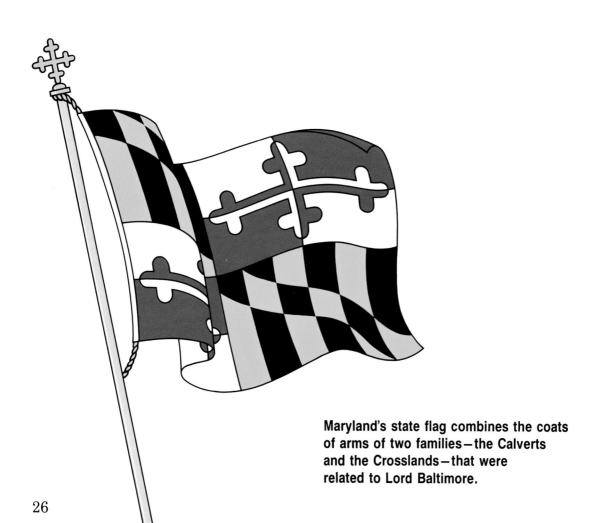

Maryland's state flag combines the coats of arms of two families—the Calverts and the Crosslands—that were related to Lord Baltimore.

Britain lost the Revolution in 1783. After the war, the former colonies agreed to create one nation. On April 28, 1788, Maryland became the seventh state to join the newly formed United States. Three years later, Maryland gave the new nation land for a capital city—Washington, D.C.

Not long after the Revolution, the War of 1812 broke out between the United States and Britain. Some American ships had been delivering goods to France, Britain's enemy. To prevent the goods from reaching the French, the British captured the American ships and forced 10,000 U.S. sailors to join the British navy.

Before the War of 1812, the British captured U.S. seamen and forced them to join the British navy.

The United States launched an attack against British land holdings in Canada and against British ships at sea. In 1814 the British attacked Washington, D. C., and planned to invade Baltimore, Maryland's largest town.

The people of Baltimore were ready. Citizens had strengthened Fort McHenry, a star-shaped fort that guarded Baltimore's harbor. Merchants sank their own ships in the harbor's channel to block British ships from the city. When the Battle of Baltimore was over, the city still belonged to Maryland.

The war ended in 1814. Afterward, Marylanders began building transportation routes. Travel and trade increased with new roads, railroads, and canals.

A Key Night in Baltimore

At 7:00 A.M. on September 13, 1814, in the pouring rain, the British opened fire on Fort McHenry. The *Terror,* the *Volcano,* and 14 other warships hurled 200-pound bombs at the fort all day and long into the following night.

Francis Scott Key, a lawyer from Maryland, watched the bombardment from an enemy ship. In the rain and dark, he couldn't tell who was winning the battle. But the next morning, an American flag was still flying high over the fort. Key knew then that the British hadn't captured Baltimore.

On the back of an old letter he had in his pocket, Key wrote a poem describing what he had seen. His poem, "The Star-Spangled Banner," later became the national anthem of the United States.

29

In the early 1800s, Marylanders began building transportation routes to carry both people and supplies west across the Appalachian Mountains. On the National Road, a route paved with stones, pioneers could travel 500 miles (800 km) from Cumberland, Maryland, to Vandalia, Illinois. Later, the Baltimore Turnpike *(top left)* and other roads were added to the famous route, which now extends from Washington, D.C., to St. Louis, Missouri.

In 1828 Marylanders began digging the Chesapeake and Ohio Canal *(bottom left)*. The canal was to connect the Potomac and Ohio rivers but was never completed. Mules towed boats loaded with goods along the trade route, which ran between Washington, D.C., and Cumberland, Maryland.

Also in 1828, the nation's first railroad company, the Baltimore and Ohio, started laying tracks west from Baltimore. One of the first trains to run the tracks was a steam locomotive with ornate coaches.

During the early 1800s, Marylanders continued to raise tobacco on plantations that were worked by slaves. A large number of slaves, most of whom were black and from Africa, lived in Maryland.

Most white Marylanders, however, did not live on plantations. Many were farmers who had small plots of land. They plowed their own fields and planted their own crops. Miners dug coal from the Appalachian Mountains. Baltimoreans sewed clothes or laid railroad tracks. Many of these people thought slavery was wrong.

Over the years, the Northern and Southern states disagreed about slavery and many other issues. The Northern states had outlawed slavery, and they wanted the Southern states to do the same. But politicians in the South refused. They argued that plantations needed slaves to make a profit.

In 1861 Southern states decided to form their own country, the Confederate States of America. In the Confederacy, slavery was legal. Troops from the North (the Union army) soon attacked the South to keep it from breaking away from the United States. Maryland was caught in the middle. Many Marylanders supported the Southern states but also wanted to keep the Union together.

The states of Virginia and Maryland surrounded Washington, D.C., the U.S. capital. Virginia had already joined the Confederacy. If Maryland joined too, Washington, D.C., would be fenced in by Confederate states.

The Union army stationed troops throughout Maryland and the U.S. capital. Pressured by the presence of Union soldiers, Maryland—a Southern state—remained in the Union. Families in Maryland were divided. During the conflict that became known as the Civil War, some people joined the Union army while others decided to fight for the Confederacy.

During the Civil War, some slaves escaped from bondage and fled to Maryland, a Union state.

The Battle of Antietam

One of the bloodiest battles in U.S. history was fought in 1862 near Sharpsburg, Maryland, at Antietam Creek. In one day, more than 23,000 soldiers were wounded or killed before the North claimed victory. Shortly after the Battle of Antietam, U.S. president Abraham Lincoln declared that all Southern slaves were free.

Abraham Lincoln *(center)*

34

The war continued until 1865, when the Confederacy surrendered. Afterward, many freed slaves moved to Maryland and to other states that had sided with the Union. In Baltimore hundreds of schools were set up to teach former slaves, most of whom had been denied an education. They learned to read and write and took jobs as factory workers or farmhands.

Black people had gained some freedoms, but many white people still treated African Americans unfairly. In Maryland and in other states, some people tried to keep blacks from getting an education or a job.

After the Civil War, many people worked in coal mines. Coal became one of the state's major products.

In 1904 a fire raged through Baltimore, destroying most of the city. Although more than 70 city blocks and 2,500 businesses went up in flames, no one died in the blaze.

During the early 1900s, industry in Maryland began to thrive. Workers produced cloth or canned oysters in Baltimore's factories, and the city became famous for the large number of straw hats it produced. The B&O Railroad carried carloads of Baltimore's products westward to be sold in other states.

Maryland's industries soon played an important role in helping U.S. soldiers fighting in foreign countries. During World War I (1914–1918), Marylanders built ships and airplanes and sewed thousands of uniforms for the military.

In the early 1900s, many Marylanders worked with oysters, either shucking, canning, or shipping the profitable seafood.

During World War II, Maryland's shipbuilding companies expanded to help the military.

DRYDOCK NO.8
(FROM ROOF OF CONTROL HOUSE)

To follow battle plans during World War II (1939–1945), U.S. troops used more than 30,000 maps drawn by government mapmakers in Maryland. Factories in the state again turned to making ships and airplanes. The state's population grew rapidly as people from other parts of the country came to work in Maryland's factories.

During the 1950s and 1960s, African Americans tried to gain the same rights that white people had. During this movement for **civil rights,** or personal freedoms, people in Maryland and across the United States protested laws that were unfair to black people.

Widespread protesting led the U.S. government to pass laws that gave black people the same rights as white people. But the struggle continues. Marylanders are still working to solve problems that exist between blacks and whites in schools and at the workplace.

In 1963 at the courthouse in Cambridge, Maryland, black youths prayed for equal rights.

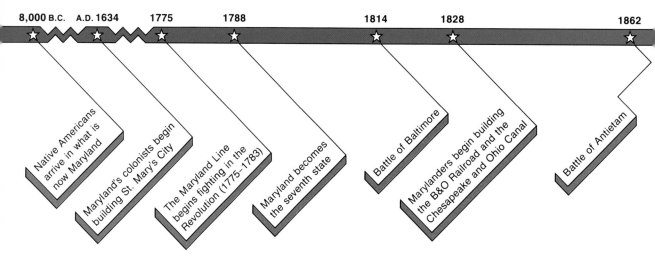

8,000 B.C. A.D. 1634 1775 1788 1814 1828 1862

Native Americans arrive in what is now Maryland

Maryland's colonists begin building St. Mary's City

The Maryland Line begins fighting in the Revolution (1775–1783)

Maryland becomes the seventh state

Battle of Baltimore

Marylanders begin building the B&O Railroad and the Chesapeake and Ohio Canal

Battle of Antietam

For thousands of years, Maryland has attracted many people. Indians may have been drawn to the area by the beauty of the mountains, the rivers, and the bay. Colonists came for religious freedom, and still others came for jobs. The state still attracts newcomers, and Maryland's population continues to grow in the 1990s.

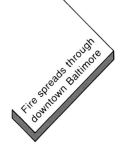

1904
Fire spreads through downtown Baltimore

1954
Black students and white students begin attending the same schools

1980
Harborplace opens on Baltimore's Inner Harbor

Inner Harbor in Baltimore is one of the world's largest natural harbors. A convention center, an aquarium, and Harborplace—a waterfront shopping arcade—attract visitors to the area.

41

Living and Working in Maryland

Nearly five million people call Maryland home. Maryland's most populated cities and suburbs—Baltimore, Silver Spring, Dundalk, and Bethesda—are located in a crowded stretch of land that runs from Baltimore to Washington, D.C. Eighty percent of Maryland's residents live within this strip.

Many Marylanders have European ancestors. In the 1700s and 1800s, most Maryland-bound **immigrants** (newcomers) carried their suitcases off boats that sailed from Great Britain and Germany. In the late 1800s, Italian, Russian, and Polish neighborhoods popped up in Baltimore.

Some of Maryland's beaches turn into castles during the state's sand-sculpture contests.

43

Since the 1960s, many Spanish-speaking immigrants have arrived from Central American countries such as El Salvador. Nearly 25 percent of Maryland's residents are African Americans. Less than 1 percent of the state's population is Native American. Most are descendants

of the Indians who lived by the Chesapeake Bay in the 1600s.

Ethnic neighborhoods, museums, theaters, and historical sites make Baltimore the artistic and historic center of the state. But Maryland's past can be found in almost every city and town.

Harbor lights brighten Baltimore's evening skyline *(right)*. **At the Afram Festival** *(facing page)*, **girls carry baskets just as their African ancestors might have carried water jugs—on their heads.**

A Baltimore Oriole gets ready to knock the ball out of the baseball park.

In St. Michaels, history buffs can stop by the Chesapeake Bay Maritime Museum to learn about people and ships that have sailed the bay. In central and western Maryland, visitors can tour Civil War battlefields or famous homes and buildings in which presidents George Washington and Abraham Lincoln were guests.

Annapolis, the state capital, features a historic capitol building. The State House has been in use for more than 200 years—longer than any other capitol building in the nation. Many of the houses in Annapolis are also quite old. They were built before the revolutionary war.

During the summer, thousands of Marylanders watch the Baltimore Orioles swat baseballs at Oriole Park. Many people sail the Chesapeake Bay, or they fish the streams and lakes in western Maryland. In the winter, skiers wind down the slopes of the Appalachian Mountains, while hockey fans watch the Skipjacks shoot a puck across the ice at Baltimore Arena.

Two horses—each being pressed to win the Preakness Stakes—run neck and neck toward the finish line.

Each May, at the Pimlico Race Course in Baltimore, select Thoroughbred horses compete in the Preakness Stakes, one of the most famous horse races in the world.

Other races aren't so serious. The Crab Derby is held every September in Crisfield. Onlookers wonder whose blue crab will skittle across the finish line first!

Rows of students stand at attention on the parade grounds of the U.S. Naval Academy.

Education has been important in Maryland since the colonial days. St. John's College, which is nearly 300 years old, became Maryland's first public, or free, school. The Peabody Institute, the nation's oldest music school, is part of Johns Hopkins University. Since before the Civil War, the U.S. Naval Academy in Annapolis has trained students to become naval officers.

More than 60 percent of Maryland's workers have jobs that provide services to people. Doctors and nurses care for hospital patients. Salespeople sell cars, vacuum cleaners, boats, and clothing. Police patrol city streets.

Government jobs are also service jobs, and another 20 percent of Maryland's population works for the government. Many national research centers—such as the National Institutes of Health, Goddard Space Flight Center, and Beltsville Agricultural Research Center—are located in Maryland. The scientists who work at these centers study everything from human diseases to insects.

Other Marylanders work for the U.S. government in Washington, D.C. They commute to jobs at the Smithsonian Institution, the Department of Defense, or any one of the hundreds of government offices in Washington.

At the Agricultural Research Center, some scientists inspect soybean plants damaged by air pollution.

Workers in a food-processing plant squeeze cucumbers into cans.

In Baltimore, Cumberland, Hagerstown, and other cities in Maryland, factories hire people to make steel, build ships, or produce gasoline. Other workers sew clothing, process sugar, or work at printing companies. Some residents of the Eastern Shore pack seafood and vegetables into cans or frozen food containers. Manufacturing employs about 9 percent of Maryland's work force.

More people work in factories than on farms, but agriculture is still important to Maryland. On the Eastern Shore, farmers grow vegetables, and they raise chickens in long, low buildings called poultry houses. Tobacco still thrives in southern Maryland. In the western part of the state, farmers raise cows, tend fruit orchards, or tap maple trees for syrup.

Coal is a major resource in western Maryland. Miners dig coal, which is used to heat homes and businesses, out of huge pits called strip mines. In other parts of the

Peach orchards thrive in western Maryland.

state, workers mine limestone, sand, and gravel, which are used to make roads and buildings.

51

Sailboats on the Chesapeake Bay catch the ocean breezes.

Fishing is a year-round job in Maryland. Blue crabs, clams, striped bass (called rockfish in Maryland), bluefin tuna, and flounder are caught by the ton. Marylanders also dredge for oysters, hauling in more shellfish than any other state.

Only 1 percent of all Marylanders work on the Chesapeake Bay. But oysters and crabs, fishing, sailboats, and the big Chesapeake Bay are what many Marylanders picture when they think of their home state.

Baltimore's Lexington Market offers a variety of seafood to Marylanders.

Boats of the Bay

Over the past 300 years, creative Marylanders have built sailboats found nowhere else in the world. These boats were designed especially for the men and women, called **watermen,** who make their living gathering oysters from the bay.

When British settlers came to Maryland in the 1600s, they found Native Americans fishing from canoes made of hollowed-out logs. To make the canoes glide more swiftly, the settlers added sails. Later, the sailboats were enlarged, and a wooden platform was added. Watermen, who had been using the boats for oystering, called them brogans.

In the 1860s, watermen began using dredges, big iron rakes, to scrape oysters from the bottom of the bay. To pull these heavy dredges over the oyster beds, watermen needed a more powerful boat. The brogan was made bigger and stronger. No one knows exactly why, but the watermen called this new boat a bugeye.

The canoe was the first craft used on the bay for gathering oysters.

The brogan had three sails and a flat bottom.

The skipjack developed in the early 1890s. Like the bugeye, the skipjack was made for oyster dredging. But the skipjack, smaller and simpler than the bugeye, was cheaper to build.

By law, watermen must use sailboats—not motorboats—to dredge oysters from the bay. So the graceful skipjacks still sail in Maryland, dragging their dredges across the bay.

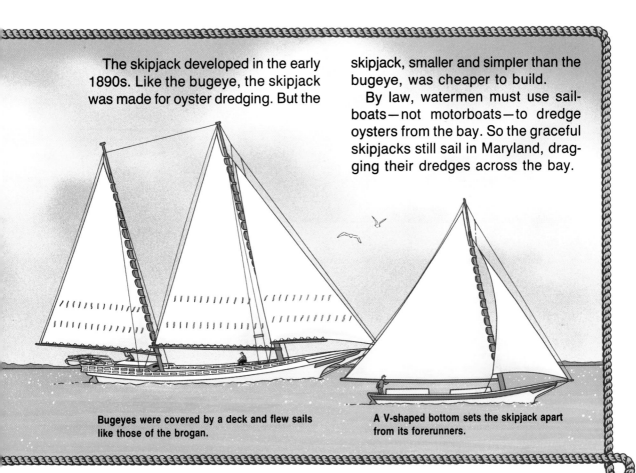

Bugeyes were covered by a deck and flew sails like those of the brogan.

A V-shaped bottom sets the skipjack apart from its forerunners.

Protecting the Environment

Many Marylanders live near one of their state's most unique natural features, the Chesapeake Bay. The bay is an **estuary**—a place where river and ocean meet. Fresh river water and salty ocean water mix in the Chesapeake Bay, the largest estuary in the United States.

The Chesapeake Bay is shallow in some places. The mixture of fresh water and saltwater in these shallow areas once made the bay a perfect home for more than 2,700 different kinds of plants and animals. But the bay is not as perfect a home as it once was.

Over the years, many **pollutants,** or harmful wastes, have entered the bay. Nitrogen and phosphorus are two pollutants that have built up in the bay. They reach the Chesapeake from several sources.

Animals such as
hermit crabs *(above)*,
which live in empty
seashells, are leaving
the bay or being killed
by pollution. As more
and more sea animals
move elsewhere, the
bay's fishers *(right)*
catch less seafood.

Nitrogen and phosphorus are found in household soaps and in lawn and garden fertilizers. Water carries soaps and fertilizers through drains, into sewers, and into rivers that enter the bay.

Too much nitrogen and phosphorus in the bay causes plants called algae to "bloom," or grow very rapidly in the water. Thick mats of algae float near the bay's surface and prevent sunlight from reaching plants living on the bottom of the bay. Without enough sunlight, these plants die, and the bay's fish lose an important source of food.

Rain washes fertilizers from cropland into nearby rivers.

When the floating algae die and decay, large amounts of oxygen are taken from the water, leaving little for the animals in the bay. Many sea animals eventually leave the bay or die.

Toxic waste also pollutes the Chesapeake Bay. Toxic waste includes poisonous metals, such as lead and mercury, and chemicals. Factories use toxic metals and chemicals to make products. Factories sometimes release toxic pollutants into the air through smokestacks. Rainfall carries these floating pollutants to streams and rivers, some of which flow into the bay. Toxic waste also comes from some paints and from some oils and gasolines that wash off city streets.

As toxic waste sinks, it is absorbed or eaten by the bay's living things, poisoning and often killing the plants and animals. People and fish-eating birds, such as bald eagles or osprey, can be harmed by eating poisoned fish.

Sometimes pollutants go through sewage treatment plants, where wastewater is cleaned before being released into rivers. But sewage treatment plants cannot remove all the toxics from wastewater, and most plants cannot remove any nitrogen or phosphorus.

Sediment, or loose soil, is another problem for the Chesapeake Bay. When people cut down trees to clear land for construction, the soil is no longer protected from harsh rains. Dirt washes into nearby creeks, rivers, and marshes that reach the Chesapeake Bay. Large amounts of sediment cloud the Chesapeake Bay's waters, fill its channels, and smother its plants and animals.

Maryland is working with the states of Virginia and Pennsylvania and with the U.S. government to clean up the bay. People are trying to keep nitrogen, phosphorus, toxic waste, and sediments out of the bay. Scientists are researching the most efficient way to treat sewage, and organizations are making sure factories limit their toxic waste.

Some organizations are providing new homes for fish. Crews in Maryland and Virginia are "planting" oysters in new beds and releasing young fish in the less-polluted parts of the bay.

Every river within a 64,000-square-mile (165,760-sq-km) range of the Chesapeake eventually flows into the bay, so even people who live far from its shores can help keep it clean. For example, people in New York State can take care not to spill oil on the ground. And city planners in Pennsylvania can keep some trees on construction sites. Whether in Maryland or a nearby state, many people can help to save the Chesapeake Bay.

Maryland's Famous People

ACTIVISTS

Frederick Douglass (1818–1895) was born a slave in Tuckahoe, Maryland. As a young man, he escaped from his master. Douglass spent the rest of his life protesting slavery. He started an antislavery newspaper called the *North Star*.

Harriet Tubman (1821–1913), from Bucktown, Maryland, escaped from slavery and fled to the North when she was about 28 years old. Tubman returned to the South 19 times, risking her life to lead more than 300 slaves to freedom.

▲ FREDERICK DOUGLASS

HARRIET TUBMAN ▶

JOHN WILKES BOOTH ▶

ACTORS

John Wilkes Booth (1838–1865), born near Bel Air, Maryland, began acting on stage at age 17. Booth, a well-known performer, became even more famous as the man who shot and killed President Abraham Lincoln in 1865. After the assassination, Booth escaped to Virginia, where he was later shot to death in a barn.

Goldie Hawn (born 1945) is an actress and comedienne who grew up in Takoma Park, Maryland. From 1968 to 1970, Hawn appeared in the TV comedy "Rowan and Martin's Laugh-In." She has acted in many movies, including *Cactus Flower* and *Bird on a Wire*.

◀ GOLDIE HAWN

Brooks Robinson (born 1937) was a third baseman with the Baltimore Orioles from 1955 to 1977. During his baseball career, Robinson won 12 Sporting News Gold Glove awards and played in 4 World Series.

◀ BROOKS ROBINSON

George ("Babe") Ruth (1895–1948) has been called the most famous person in American sports history. Born in Baltimore, Ruth began his baseball career at age 19 with the Baltimore Orioles. Ruth went on to play for the New York Yankees and became known for his powerful home runs.

Johnny Unitas (born 1933) was a quarterback for the Baltimore Colts football team for 16 years. Unitas won three Super Bowls with the Colts, set many records in his career, and was named to the Pro Football Hall of Fame in 1979.

BABE RUTH ▶

◀ JOHNNY UNITAS

JOHNS HOPKINS ▶

BUSINESS LEADERS

Johns Hopkins (1795–1873) grew up in Anne Arundel County, Maryland. He helped create the B&O Railroad. At his death, Hopkins left $7 million to build the Johns Hopkins University and Johns Hopkins Hospital in Maryland.

Enoch Pratt (1808–1896) moved to Baltimore in 1831. His business interests included banking, insurance, and transportation. Pratt invested much of his money in public projects, including the Enoch Pratt Free Library in Baltimore.

Eubie Blake (1883–1983) was born in Baltimore. A pioneer of ragtime music, Blake wrote "I'm Just Wild About Harry" and "Memories of You," songs that were popular in the early 1900s. He died at the age of 100.

Billie Holiday (1915–1959), from Baltimore, was one of the most popular singers in jazz history. In 1927 Holiday moved to New York, where she began singing in clubs and recording music. Her style has influenced many singers.

◀ BILLIE HOLIDAY

BENJAMIN BANNEKER ▶

▲ FRANCIS PEYTON ROUS

THURGOOD MARSHALL ▶

SCIENTISTS

Benjamin Banneker (1731–1806) lived all his life on the farm where he was born near Baltimore County, Maryland. He taught himself mathematics and astronomy. Banneker helped lay out the boundaries of the city of Washington, D.C. He also published several almanacs—books that included weather predictions for the upcoming year.

Francis Peyton Rous (1879–1970) was born in Baltimore. His early studies of chicken viruses are now used by cancer researchers. For his discoveries, Rous won the 1966 Nobel Prize in medicine.

SUPREME COURT JUSTICES

Thurgood Marshall (1908–1993), from Baltimore, graduated at the head of his law-school class at Howard University in Washington, D.C. As a lawyer, Marshall argued and won court cases that gave black people more civil rights. In 1967 Marshall became the first black judge on the U.S. Supreme Court.

Roger Brooke Taney (1777–1864), a native of Calvert County, Maryland, was the chief justice of the U.S. Supreme Court from 1836 to 1864. In one of Taney's most famous decisions, the Dred Scott case, he ruled that the U.S. government could not outlaw slavery in the western territories.

◀ ROGER
BROOKE
TANEY

WRITERS

H. L. MENCKEN ▶

Dashiell Hammett (1894–1961), born in St. Mary's County, Maryland, wrote detective stories, including *The Maltese Falcon* and *The Thin Man* series. Many of his books were made into movies.

Frances Ellen Watkins Harper (1825–1911), an author and speech-maker, began writing poetry as a teenager. She spoke out against slavery and rallied for women's rights. Harper, who was born in Baltimore, was the first black person in America to have a short story published.

H. L. Mencken (1880–1956) wrote humorous stories about Americans. Born in Baltimore, Mencken began his career as a newspaper reporter. He eventually wrote many books, essays, and articles.

◀ UPTON
SINCLAIR

Upton Sinclair (1878–1968), born in Baltimore, wrote at least 90 books, hundreds of articles, and many plays. One of Sinclair's best-known novels, *The Jungle*, brought attention to some of the nation's social problems, including the difficult lives of factory workers in the early 1900s.

Facts-at-a-Glance

Nickname: Old Line State
Song: "Maryland, My Maryland"
Motto: *Fatti Maschii Parole Femine*
   (Manly Deeds, Womanly Words)
Flower: black-eyed Susan
Tree: white oak
Bird: Baltimore oriole

Population: 4,781,468*
Rank in population, nationwide: 19th
Area: 12,407 sq mi (32,134 sq km)
Rank in area, nationwide: 42nd
Date and ranking of statehood:
   April 28, 1788; the 7th state
Capital: Annapolis (33,187*)
Major cities (and populations*):
   Baltimore (736,014), Silver Spring (76,046),
   Dundalk (65,800), Bethesda (62,936),
   Columbia (75,886)
U.S. senators: 2
U.S. representatives: 8
Electoral votes: 10

Places to visit: Afro-American Heritage Museum in Marshall's Corner, Cranesville Subarctic Swamp near Oakland, St. Mary's City near Leonardtown, National Aquarium in Baltimore, Star-Spangled Banner Flag House in Baltimore

Annual events: Maryland Kite Festival near Baltimore (April), Preakness Stakes in Baltimore (May), Sand Sculpture Contest in Ocean City (June), State Jousting Championships (Aug.–Oct.), St. Mary's County Oyster Festival near Leonardtown (Oct.), Maryland Christmas Show in Frederick (Nov.)

*1990 census

Average January temperature: 33° F (1° C)   **Average July temperature:** 75° F (24° C)

Natural resources: loam and clay soils, sand and gravel, granite, limestone, coal, natural gas, talc

Agricultural products: broilers, milk, corn, soybeans, beef cattle, tobacco, apples, cucumbers, snap beans, tomatoes

Manufactured products: electrical machinery, food products, paint, soap, fertilizers, printed materials, metals, transportation equipment

ENDANGERED SPECIES
Mammals—sei whale, gray wolf, snowshoe hare, Indiana bat, humpback whale
Birds—Northern goshawk, upland sandpiper, ivory-billed woodpecker, piping plover
Reptiles—Atlantic leatherback turtle, mountain earth snake, Atlantic hawksbill turtle
Fish—shortnose sturgeon, longnose sucker
Plants—flattened spikerush, sea milkwort, potato dandelion, pondspice, Barbara's buttons

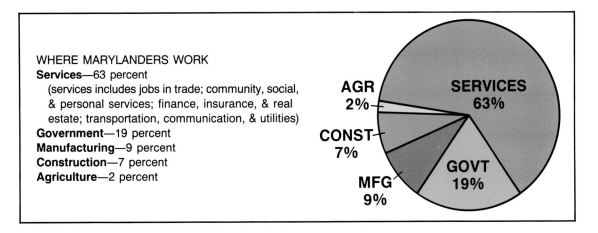

WHERE MARYLANDERS WORK
Services—63 percent
(services includes jobs in trade; community, social, & personal services; finance, insurance, & real estate; transportation, communication, & utilities)
Government—19 percent
Manufacturing—9 percent
Construction—7 percent
Agriculture—2 percent

AGR 2%
SERVICES 63%
CONST 7%
GOVT 19%
MFG 9%

PRONUNCIATION GUIDE

Antietam (an-TEET-uhm)

Appalachian (ap-uh-LAY-chuhn)

Assateague (AS-uh-TEEG)

Chesapeake (CHEHS-uh-PEEK)

Choptank (CHAHP-tangk)

Nanticoke (NAN-tih-kohk)

Patapsco (puh-TAP-skoh)

Piscataway (pihs-KAT-uh-way)

Pocomoke (POH-kuh-mohk)

Potomac (puh-TOH-mihk)

Susquehanna (suhs-kwuh-HAN-uh)

Wicomico (wy-KAHM-uh-koh)

Glossary

civil rights The right of all citizens—regardless of race, religion, sex—to enjoy life, liberty, property, and equal protection under the law.

colony A territory ruled by a country some distance away.

estuary An ocean inlet in which fresh river water mixes with salty ocean water.

Great Lakes A chain of five lakes in Canada and the northern United States. They are Lakes Superior, Michigan, Huron, Erie, and Ontario.

immigrant A person who moves into a foreign country and settles there.

marsh A spongy wetland soaked with water for long periods of time. Marshes are usually treeless; grasses are the main form of vegetation.

plantation A large estate, usually in a warm climate, on which crops are grown by workers who live on the estate. In the past, plantation owners often used slave labor.

pollutant A substance that dirties or poisons a natural resource, such as air or water.

sediment Solid materials—such as soil, sand, and minerals—that are carried into a body of water by wind, ice, or running water.

toxic waste A poisonous material that contaminates the environment and that can cause death, disease, or other defects.

waterman A person who earns his or her living by fishing, gathering oysters, or working at other jobs on the water.

Index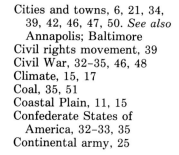

Acknowledgments:

Maryland Cartographics, Inc., pp. 2, 11; John Elder, MD DNR, pp. 2–3, 9 (right); Jayson Knott, MD DNR, pp. 6, 58; Jack Lindstrom, p. 7; Middleton Evans, pp. 8–9, 14, 16, 17, 41, 43, 44, 48, 52, 53, 57 (right), 61; Doyen Salsig, p. 10; Maryland Department of Agriculture, pp. 12, 23, 50, 51, 69; Craig Phillips, p. 13; Lisa Green, p. 15; Prints and Photographs Division, Maryland Historical Society, pp. 18–19, 20, 21, 24, 29 (bottom), 30 (top left), 34 (left), 35, 37, 64 (bottom center); Virginia State Library and Archives, p. 22; Virginia State Library and Archives/The Company of Military Historians, p. 25; Chicago Historical Society, pp. 28, 33; Library of Congress, pp. 29 (top right), 62 (top right, bottom right), 64 (bottom right), 65 (center, right); Smithsonian Institution, Photo #83–7221, p. 29 (top left); Maryland State Archives, MdHR G 1477–6404, p. 30 (bottom left); Historical Pictures Service—Chicago, pp. 30–31; National Archives, pp. 34 (right), 65 (bottom left); Allegany County Historical Society, p. 35 (bottom left); Enoch Pratt Free Library, p. 36; Baltimore Museum of Industry, p. 38; UPI/Bettmann, p. 39; James Blank/Root Resources, p. 45; Jerry Wachter/Baltimore Orioles, p. 46; Double J Photos/Pimlico Race Course, p. 47; Agricultural Research Service/USDA, p. 49; Michael J. Reber, Chesapeake Biological Laboratory, p. 57 (left); National Park Service, p. 62 (top left); Hollywood Book & Poster Company, pp. 62 (bottom left), 64 (right); Baltimore Orioles, p. 63 (top left); National Baseball Library, Cooperstown, New York, p. 63 (top right); Independent Picture Service, p. 63 (bottom left, bottom right); Nobel Foundation, p. 64 (bottom left); Jean Matheny, p. 66; Robert O'Connor, Washington County Convention and Visitors Bureau, p. 70.